WATCH AND PRAY:

Be Ready

(Second Edition)

THE RAPTURE

- ✦ What is it?
- ✦ When Will it Occur?

THE BOOK OF REVELATION

Glenna Hartzog

Watch and Pray: Be Ready.
Copyright © 2016 by Glenna Hartzog.
Copyright © 2019 by Glenna Hartzog, *Second Edition.*

This publication contains the opinions and ideas of its author. It is intended to provide helpful and informative material on the subjects addressed in the publication. The author and publisher specifically disclaim all responsibility for any liability, loss, or risk, personal or otherwise, which is incurred as a consequence, directly or indirectly, of the use and application of any of the contents of this book.

All scripture references are from the King James Version (KJV) of the Bible unless otherwise stated. Italics are for emphasis by the author.

ISBN: 978-1-950850-14-3   [Paperback Edition]
         978-1-951742-10-2   [Hardback Edition]
         978-1-950850-17-4   [eBook Edition]

Printed and bound in The United States of America.

Published by

The Mulberry Books, LLC.
8330 E Quincy Avenue,
Denver CO 80237
themulberrybooks.com

Mark 13:32 – 33, 35 – 37

32 But of that day and that hour knoweth no man, no, not the angels which are in heaven, neither the Son, but the Father.

33 Take ye heed, *watch and pray*: for ye know not when the time is.

35 *Watch ye therefore: for ye know not when the master of the house cometh, at even, or at midnight, or at the cockcrowing, or in the morning:*

36 Lest coming suddenly he find you sleeping.

37 And what I say unto you I say unto all, *Watch*.

CONTENTS

PREFACE

The following will be covered in this book:

- ✤ Definition of terms: In this text, I will show you from the scripture what occurs at the time of the rapture, and I will compare the two major teachings on the rapture. I will explain what is meant by pre-trib and post-trib rapture.
- ✤ I will go back over these scriptures and others and discuss how the scripture fits into pre- and/or post-trib teaching on the rapture.
- ✤ The audience will be varied. Some are more schooled and defining terms will seem very basic. For others who have not learned about the rapture, this information is most necessary. Either way, it will be helpful for all of us to recognize the terms in the same way.
- ✤ I will take you through the book of Revelation and give some insights that may help you be more comfortable in reading and understanding this book laden with mysterious and strange images. I will also show you a great way to organize the material by the sequence of events instead of a chronological order of chapters.

Revelation 1:3

3 Blessed is he that readeth, and they that hear the words of this prophecy, and keep those things which are written therein: for the time is at hand.

The more you read the book of Revelation and look into it and come to understand it, the less intimidating it will be.

The most important point that I will make throughout this book is italicized in the following text:

Mark 13:32 – 33, 35 – 37

32 But of that day and that hour knoweth no man, no, not the angels which are in heaven, neither the Son, but the Father.

33 Take ye heed, *watch and pray:* for ye know not when the time is.

35 *Watch ye therefore: for ye know not when the master of the house cometh, at even, or at midnight, or at the cockcrowing, or in the morning:*

36 Lest coming suddenly he find you sleeping.

37 And what I say unto you I say unto all, *Watch.*

I am using the King James Version throughout the text unless otherwise stated. I am not King James only, but like to use it as a standard. Many words are archaic and not used the same today as they were centuries ago, so I will sometimes explain what the word would be if translated today. I may quote the meaning of a word from the Strong's Concordance, which gives definitions of the original Greek or Hebrew word.

In verse 32 of Mark 13, we are told that no man knows the day or the hour that Jesus is returning. In verse 33, it speaks to the importance to "watch and pray." This is one of the aspects of being ready. Verse 35 is the scripture I will be emphasizing throughout the text. "Whether at even, or at midnight, or at the cock crowing (rooster crowning), or in the morning," *whenever* the rapture is, we are to watch and pray to be ready. There are many theories, teachings, and ideas. We need to recognize that if things are different than what we have come to believe that there is a scriptural answer and the prophecies in the Bible endure.

In this study text, you will see a biblical basis for supporting a rapture that is post-trib. Very few people in the church today ever hear a teaching on this perspective. The majority of the church world today holds to the pre-tribulation (pre-trib) rapture teaching. Even movies have been made showing a pre-trib rapture. If this teaching is correct, then it will be a wonderful occasion, in which those who are born again (born of the Spirit) will not only be changed to an immortal (eternal, resurrected) body, but also miss the horrible time that the rest of the world will experience during what is known as the Great Tribulation.

Matthew 24:21

21 For then shall be great tribulation, such as
was not since the beginning of the world to
this time, no, nor ever shall be.

With a law of risks and benefits, it behooves all believers to take a look at the possibility of a post-trib rapture. If you are convinced that the rapture is before the tribulation, you risk being caught by surprise if you find yourself having to face the Tribulation period. (Most people who believe in a pre-trib rapture do so because they have been taught it that way. It is what they have always heard, and they just cannot see it any other way.) A person who has gained an understanding of a biblical foundation for a post-trib rapture benefits from the knowledge and will be more prepared than the one who will not recognize potential inaccuracies in strongly held positions. The person who believes in a post-trib rapture has nothing to lose if the rapture is before the Tribulation period. Everyone will be shouting so happy to miss what is coming on the earth including those who thought it was going to be post-trib. In fact, those who believe in a post-tribulation rapture may be shouting even louder.

If, however, the rapture is after the tribulation, those who are so insistent that it is before, could become very confused and insist that things are not as they seem. I can just hear some saying, "This can't be the mark of the beast because we haven't been raptured yet, and we aren't even supposed to know who the antichrist is." Many who received the teaching will become disillusioned and many could end up in a panic not knowing what to do. This is what I mean by the law of risks and benefits. Just as with the atheist wanting a believer to prove God exists: It is the atheist who takes great risk for not finding out if there really is a God. It is believers who have the most to benefit. It is more important for the atheist to learn if there is a God because he is the one who has the most to lose. He will have to stand before God and face the judgment. If there is no God, the believer in Jesus, who follows His teaching of love and the golden rule (doing unto others as you would have them do unto you), will live a great life, then die with nothing to lose and therefore, no risk. The believer has heaven to gain because there is a God.

By learning this biblical perspective, it will help you to be prepared and understand what is happening. If we go up first, no harm. If we are here during any of the Tribulation period, things could get so hectic that there wouldn't be time to go through a thorough teaching. Learning it now, could mean a great deal.

If you believe in a pre-trib rapture, it will not hurt to learn a biblical post-trib perspective, even if it is just to keep it on a "back-burner".

ARE YOU READY?

I address this text to born-again believers as the biggest audience and often use the term "we" for those of us believers who are "alive and remain." Only those who are born of His Spirit (born-again) will go up in the rapture. The same Spirit it will take for us to be raptured is the same Spirit it will take to go through any trials that may come before the rapture. Either way, we have to be ready. We have to know that we are walking by His ways, that the Spirit of God is in us, that we are "new creatures" in Christ, and we are "walking in the light as He is in the light." It is going to take His Spirit to raise us up: To raise us up if we die or to take us up in the rapture. It will also take His Spirit to endure whatever we have to face in this life and remain true to Him.

If you do not know that if you died today, you will go to heaven, you can right now make the decision to turn from the way you are going, ask Jesus to forgive you of you sins, and come into your life to make you a new creature (creation). Ask Him to come into your heart by His Spirit. Turn to Him, and you can be born of His Spirit. Some may say, "I am not a bad person. I live just as good as anyone else." God has high standards, and no sin will enter heaven. If you have ever told a lie, had a bad thought toward someone, or have not been able to forgive someone, then you have sinned. "All have sinned" (Rom. 3:23).

John 3:3

3 Jesus answered and said unto him, Verily, verily, I say unto thee, except a man be born again, he cannot see the kingdom of God.

Romans 10:9-10

9 That if thou shalt confess with thy mouth the Lord Jesus, and shalt believe in thine heart that God hath raised him from the dead, thou shalt be saved.

10 For with the heart man believeth unto righteousness; and with the mouth confession is made unto salvation.

Acts 3:19

19 Repent ye therefore, and be converted, that your sins may be blotted out, when the times of refreshing shall come from the presence of the Lord;

Romans 10:9 states to confess the Lord Jesus. You have to make Him Lord (boss) of your life. Ask Him to be your boss. Tell Him that you want to go His way, not yours. Jesus asked why call Him Lord and not do the things that He says (Luke 6:46). Making Him Lord is obeying His Word. You do that with the help of His Spirit. Verse 10 says with the heart you believe and with the mouth, confession is made. So if you will, in your heart, turn to the Lord. Just talk to Him about the way things are in your life: That there is sin, and you want to repent (turn from the sin) and follow Jesus. Ask Him into your heart by His Spirit. Ask Him to forgive you; tell Him that you believe

He was raised from the dead. You can be forgiven and saved through His blood that He shed for you.

God's heart is for people to be saved and live for eternity with Him. Satan's desire is to take as many people to the lake of fire with him as he can.

We need to be ready for *whenever* the rapture is. The church needs to be gearing for a great time of revival and evangelism, instead of the mindset that nothing can happen, and we will just disappear and miss any trouble. Many may flock to the churches for answers, filled with fear and despair, and hungry to find God.

If we are not caught up in the fear and despair, we will be able to lead many to saving faith in Jesus.

CHAPTER 1

Laying a Foundation

WATCH AND PRAY

It was the last night of Jesus' time living on the earth. He and His disciples had finished the Passover meal and had gone to the Mount of Olives. Jesus had told the disciples that he would be killed. The disciples did not totally understand what they had been told. Even after Jesus' resurrection and before His ascension, they were still asking Him when the kingdom of God about which Jesus had so often spoken was going to come. Earlier, during what is known as the transfiguration, (because Jesus' and His clothing appeared white as light,) Moses and Elijah appeared with Him and spoke to Jesus in greater detail concerning the crucifixion than what Jesus had learned from Hebrew scrolls. The disciples did not hear the details.

> **Luke 9:31**
>
> 31 Who appeared in glory, and spake of his decease which he should accomplish at Jerusalem.

At the Mount of Olives, Jesus asked the disciples to watch and pray as He went away from them to pray. The disciples may have tried to pray. They may also have been thinking about other times when Jesus went off to pray and prayed all night. How long will He be this time? Inadvertently, they fell asleep. Jesus came back to them more than once and found them asleep.

Matthew 26:40 – 41

40 And he cometh unto the disciples, and findeth them asleep, and saith unto Peter, What, could ye not watch with me one hour?

41 Watch and pray, that ye enter not into temptation: the spirit indeed is willing, but the flesh is weak.

I don't think this was a rebuke. It was said out of concern. Jesus was in much distress, and He wanted His disciples to be ready for what was coming. Jesus is speaking to us across time concerning the end-time and asks, "Can you not watch and pray?" Around the world, the church can see events bringing us close to horrible times. We witness Christians getting their head sawed off (not chopped) for refusing to blaspheme the true God with the name of Allah. Yet especially in America, much of the church seems to be asleep. The attitude is that we will be caught up out of the world before America faces hard times. This leads to a defeatist attitude. Mention a terrible law being proposed that violates religious freedom, for example, and there are those who would say, "It is just the signs of the times, but not to worry, we will be raptured out soon." If a discussion goes to the fact that America could soon be judged for her sins, the comment is that we are going to have a great awakening instead. Yes, there may be a great harvest of souls in America, but it may take trouble to wake her up. Even then, many will sit back and watch a move of God and not even participate. Have you ever heard of the Brownsville revival? It was a great move of God in the 1990s in Pensacola, Florida. How many today even know about it?

Those looking for an awakening need to realize that America will not return to the days of "Leave It to Beaver" and "Father Knows Best" and small town America in which almost everyone is in church on Sunday, you don't have to lock your doors, and stores and restaurants aren't even open on Sundays.

The nation of Israel was taken into captivity by Assyria. The nation of Judah did not go into captivity to Assyria because of some good kings such as Hezekiah who brought the people back

2

to God, restored the temple and the feasts, and prayed for God's protection. Not much later, Judah was back in idolatry, and God had had enough. Judah was taken into captivity by Babylon. Jerusalem's walls were torn down, the city burned, and the temple destroyed. Gone were the glory days of David and Solomon.

Many of our leaders in America, by defying God and taking God out of America's life, are taking our country to the brink. We are being pushed off a cliff, and the church cannot seem to do anything but watch. Our glory days of being a Judeo-Christian country and the power for good in the world are almost gone. It seems that those helping us over the cliff, even though they are Americans, want to blame America for the word's evils and want to see us diminished. Anti-God, anti-American, anti-Semitic rhetoric is being openly endorsed. The battle for all that is good and right has heated up. It seems we may never be more than one election away from losing the values that were once synonymous with America. Those calling for the transformation claim the other party is the one who has lost their moral compass. It has even been said that it is not Christian to stand for life, protecting our borders and standing with law enforcement. Good is being called evil, and evil is being called good.

Isaiah 5:20

20 Woe into them that call evil good, and good evil: that put darkness for light, and light for darkness: that put bitter for sweet, and sweet for bitter.

The warning coming to us from Jesus is to watch and pray. He wants His own to be prepared to stand strong and help others who become distraught over what is coming. He said that men's hearts would fail over what comes on the earth.

Luke 21: 25 – 26

25 And there shall be signs in the sun, and in the moon, and in the stars; and upon the earth distress of nations, with perplexity; the sea and the waves roaring;

26 Men's hearts failing them for fear, and for looking after those things which are coming on the earth: for the powers of heaven shall be shaken.

Christians can be a lighthouse on a hill and a refuge, if we are not caught off guard and are ready for what is ahead by watching and praying.

UNDERSTANDING THE FUTURE

As stated in the preface, I will be reviewing the biblical foundation for a post-trib rapture and sharing highlights of the book of Revelation. I am not laying this out to be argumentative or convince anyone of anything. In fact, some may even be more convinced that what they have come to believe is the truth. I have heard on both sides that "the more I study, the more convinced I am." With the two teachings, pre- or post-trib, there are only three possibilities. Either pre-trib is correct or post-trib is correct or both are wrong. They cannot both be right. There are some who hold to a mid-trib rapture. I do not address it because the same points supporting a post-trib rapture would counter that. I love what my pastor has been saying for years. There is a pan theory. It is going to pan out the way God intends no matter how we believe it.[1]

If you are born again, the Spirit of Truth is in you. Jesus is the way, the truth, and the life (John 14:6). Jesus is truth and His Spirit leads us into truth. However, our understanding of God's truth has been filtered through a whole lifetime of cultural and religious learning. I have often said that I want truth regardless of what I have always believed. We now see through a glass darkly (1 Cor. 13:12). When we get to heaven, I can imagine us saying, "I knew that . . . why didn't I know that?" No one who has ever lived on earth but Jesus has all truth. This includes all denominations. If you are in a church that says you can only be saved if you get baptized in "this" church, then there is something wrong. We need to be open: Not to be tossed to and fro by every wind of doctrine (Eph. 4:14), but to be willing to be instructed. In Proverbs, we are told that a wise man will hear instruction.

4

Proverbs 1:5

5   A wise man will hear, and will increase
learning.

Those who are so certain that everything they have learned
and or taught is correct no matter what may find themselves very
confused or holding on to false ideas. If they are so adamant that
they are correct, they may not see what is really happening and
remain deceived.

Every generation has framed Revelation to fit their time. If I had
been around during the Second World War, I would have thought
that Hitler could very easily be the Antichrist. He definitely had
an Antichrist spirit. Just think: he tried to rule the world, and he
engaged in the "final solution," which was an attempt to kill all the
Jewish people in the world.

I read early commentary out of the Geneva translation of the
Bible, which I understand to be the one that the Pilgrims brought
with them to the new world. The commentary on Revelation is that
a day is a year in Bible prophecy, and that the twelve hundred and
sixty days (three and ½ years) in Revelation is actually years. These
years began at the time of Jesus and ended in the 13th century. One
of the popes in that century was the Antichrist. It is one thing to
teach something, but to put it into commentary in a Bible is rather
bold. You need to be aware that commentary is man's ideas. I
imagine many who read this Bible thought the commentary was a
part of the truth of God's Word because it was in their Bible.

People in every generation seem to feel theirs is the one in which
Jesus will return. This is good because it gives a sense of urgency that
we need to be getting people saved. If ours is that time in history,
finally, when all scripture will be fulfilled and Jesus will return, it is
an exciting time to be in!

Many ministers who feel called to eschatology (study of end-
time events) may feel that since they are called to teach on it that
God would give answers to all their questions. As they studied, they
filled in the blanks or thought an idea they had must be revelation

from God since He called them to teach on it. There are as many ideas as there are teachers. Some may be correct, but which ones? How do we know what is right? What we can do is read and pray and be open asking God to show us truth and trusting His Spirit to reveal what we need to know when we need to know it. An important beginning for us to learn is to understand that we don't know it all. Familiarity with the Word will make it easier for us to hear and recognize truth and know when some teaching doesn't fit what the Word says. Do not be afraid of reading the Word, including Revelation, even if you don't understand very much. Don't accept everything you are taught just because you have confidence in the person teaching. Read the Word yourself. Be a Berean. In the book of Acts, the Bereans would search the scriptures to see if what they were being taught were true.

Acts 17:11

11 These were more noble than those in Thessalonica, in that they received the word with all readiness of mind, and searched the scriptures daily, whether those things were so.

I will share with you many ideas that I have seen while meditating on end-time scriptures, including Revelation. I will not state them as absolute, so you will see me saying many times, "I don't know" or "I could be wrong."

When it comes to future events, we may not be able to understand all that is happening until the time it happens, or after it happens. An event can confirm that Bible prophecy is occurring. Just think of all the prophecies concerning the coming of Jesus the first time. There is no way any scribe could have come up with the way all of the messianic prophecies would be fulfilled: Born of a virgin in Bethlehem, but come out of Egypt; be a suffering lamb to the slaughter, but be a reigning king with the government upon his shoulders. Even if someone had written a story about a woman conceiving by the Holy Spirit, going with her husband to Bethlehem because of an unusual tax, Joseph being warned in a dream to flee to Egypt, then Jesus being crucified, raised, and coming back to rule and reign, who would have believed such a story as possible? Even in Jesus' day, things were muddled and confused. The disciples thought He would end Roman rule and set up His kingdom, not die, be resurrected, and ascend to heaven. At the time of the ascent as is mentioned in Acts 1, the disciples asked Jesus when He was going to set up His kingdom. Imagine if they had known almost two thousand years would pass, and it still has not happened.

So how can we expect to understand all the details of the Second Coming of Christ, the rapture and everything John saw in Revelation? It is becoming more and more evident that in order to understand end-times and the book of Revelation, it is going to take revelation from God. We need to spiritually discern and learn by revelation. As end-time events get closer and closer, it may be time or soon time for God to begin to show us these things. John was given words and told not to write them down and was given a book to eat. Daniel was told there would be things that would not be revealed until the end (Dan. 12:4). As these things start to be revealed, we want to be in a position because of our familiarity with the Word, to recognize truth when we hear it. Technological advances help us recognize more today than when John wrote the Book of Revelation. Then again, there may be some end-time events that we will not understand until they happen, but we will be able to recognize the prophetic significance.

As the time approaches and it seems the fulfilment of end-time prophecies are very near, the Lord will see fit to show His own what is happening or soon to happen to prepare us. All the charts and previous teachings may prove to be right, somewhat right, or have missed the mark altogether. This text brings out some of the ways pre-trib teaching with the authoritative-looking charts have missed the mark biblically.

So many world events are occurring so quickly that it is hard to imagine there could be much more time left. Matthew 24, one of the texts we will be discussing, mentions events leading up to Jesus' coming as the "beginning of sorrows." Some translators say this is similar to the beginning of labor pains in birth. During labor, at first, the contractions are short in duration, light in strength, and far apart. As birth approaches, the contractions become longer in duration, more intense, and closer together. This is the way things look today. Things are happening so quickly. It looks as though those labor pains are getting close to the end.

The main theme of this text is to be ready, and the way to be ready is to watch and pray.

Mark 13:32 – 33, 35 – 37

32 But of that day and that hour knoweth no man, no, not the angels which are in heaven, neither the Son, but the Father.

33 Take ye heed, *watch and pray:* for ye know not when the time is.

35 *Watch ye therefore: for ye know not when the master of the house cometh, at even, or at midnight, or at the cockcrowing, or in the morning:*

36 Lest coming suddenly he find you sleeping.

37 And what I say unto you I say unto all, *Watch.*

To watch is to:

✢ Stay in the light as He is in the light. Strive to obey the Word, be quick to ask for forgiveness, and repent when you disobey,
✢ Keep your eyes on Jesus,
✢ Keep yourself in the Word, follow Him, and be obedient to what He says. (This is done by His Spirit),
✢ Pray and look to Him.

In verse (v) 35, it says the master may come at even (before the dark), at midnight (in the middle of the dark), or in the morning (at the end of the dark). So if He comes for the church—pre-trib, mid-trib, or post-trib... *whenever* it is—be ready.

Watch and pray, *whenever* it is. I have more questions than answers, which is fine, because a person cannot learn if he is certain he knows it all. With some of the questions, I have received answers, but I am willing to acknowledge that some of the answers may be wrong. I may say, "I don't know," many times. If teachers of Revelation and end-time were honest with themselves, they would admit that we really don't know. I can appreciate a minister, such as my pastor, who admits this is the case concerning much about end-times.[1]

When you read the book of Revelation fifty times in a row, which I did as one of my study time projects recently, you become aware of every phrase and word. Some have said about my questions, "I don't let things like that bother me." Well, I am not bothered by them. It is exciting. It is exciting that God can speak to us and show us answers. God has said it is given to us to know mysteries (Matt. 13:11). It is fascinating to learn even minor details, especially when you see something that you never heard before. There are some things I have seen and learned that no one has ever taught me. I never have heard anyone say it. Other times, I can recognize that a teaching fits the scripture because I am familiar with the scripture and can recognize the truth when I hear it.

Just as I have learned things, you can read, and God can reveal things to you. Do not feel you can only learn by listening to other teachers. Be willing to read and to study the Word for yourself. Then as you read, ask God for wisdom. It is good to have teachers whom God has put in the church. Why would we need to "reinvent the wheel" when the teachers can help us advance more rapidly? At the same time, we need to search the scriptures ourselves. I have said that the person who agrees 100 percent with a minister is following man and does not know God for himself. Since no one knows all truth, we may see things differently, or because of a particular life experience have a different perspective on a particular scripture. This may not mean that one or the other is wrong. A church's teaching needs to be in line with the basic foundational truths found in Hebrews.

Hebrews 6: 1-2

1 Therefore leaving the principles of the doctrine of Christ, let us go on unto perfection; not laying again the foundation of repentance from dead works, and of faith toward God,

2   Of the doctrine of baptisms, and of laying on of hands, and of resurrection of the dead, and of eternal judgment.

If you are in a church that is not teaching truth about salvation, then you need to leave that church and let God lead you to a true Bible-believing church. I have stated previously that the teaching of when the rapture occurs is not a salvation issue. No one should be argumentative about this topic. If a person cannot discuss the topic without getting belligerent, then drop it. It is not necessary to prove your point. A born-again believer can still be saved and go to heaven when he dies, or go up in the rapture no matter when he thinks it is. We just need to be open in these days to what He wants to tell us in order to follow His direction and understand what is going on. In many of rapture scriptures, we are continually warned to not be deceived.

The following are scriptures that would be good for you to read. The first four are gospel chapters that cover Jesus' answer to the question His disciples asked about when the temple would be destroyed and the sign of his coming. (These passages are what some have called the Signs of the Times. Jesus was asked what would be the sign of His coming, but along with answering that question, He also mentions many events that we could also call signs.) I include the whole chapter so you can read all the context. First Corinthians 15, 1 Thessalonians 4, and 2 Thessalonians 2 are specific scriptures about the rapture. Then, of course, I will cover the Book of Revelation. I will have these in the text so you can read them as you read the book and follow along with the discussion.

SCRIPTURES TO READ

Matthew 24	I Corinthians 15
Mark 13	I Thessalonians 4
Luke 17	II Thessalonians 2
Luke 21	Book of Revelation

This may seem like a great deal. There are twenty-two chapters in Revelation. If you read four chapters a day, you can finish in six days. Remember, we are blessed for reading Revelation. So read, even if you don't understand. Don't worry, you are not alone. The more you read and learn, the more the Holy Spirit can teach you. Ask for wisdom. The things of God must be spiritually discerned.

I Corinthians 2:14

14 But the natural man receiveth not the things of the Spirit of God: for they are foolishness unto him: neither can he know them, because they are spiritually discerned.

As a believer, we have a spiritual mind, but we still have our human physical, natural mind. We can have a natural understanding of a scripture, but it doesn't necessarily mean it is spiritually discerned. We have to hear with our spiritual ears. Because we have the Spirit of God, we can understand the scriptures better than an unbeliever, if we are in tune to the Spirit. I remember a minister saying that he gave an interview about how to receive healing by faith to a non-believer, and an article was written that distorted what he said. The minister realized that had he been teaching this to his congregation, because of the Spirit of God, they would have been able to spiritually discern it. Because the interviewer was an unbeliever, he could not understand. Beyond spiritual discernment, there is revelation knowledge in which the scripture will just "light up" with understanding, and it will seem to permeate all through the Bible.

When we read, we want to ask for the wisdom of God to spiritually discern what God is saying. Revelation knowledge will give us greater understanding of end-time scriptures as the time approaches.

HOW TO READ

The scriptures on the list will be presented throughout the text. However, it would be beneficial to be familiar with all of the scriptures in advance. Doing so will help you better recognize a concept because you have seen it before.

Try to read the scriptures without a preconceived doctrine. Lay aside the way you believe about the rapture and just read. Try not to frame the scriptures based on the preconceived idea. This is very hard to do. It is much easier to learn something the first time than to unlearn something that is wrong. If the person who wants truth were aware that a doctrine he believed was false, then the person would discard the false doctrine. If you believe a particular doctrine is correct (even if it is false), as you read the Bible, you'll make the scriptures fit the doctrine.

Preconceived ideas create circular reasoning. What I mean by this is that you believe something is true because the preconceived idea says it is true. The preconceived idea says one thing, so that must be what the scripture means. We often don't realize when we are using circular reasoning. If the preconceived idea (or premise) is correct, then great; you are framing the scriptures correctly, but if the premise is wrong, then you will frame the scriptures wrong. Some people will say they are just "rightly dividing the Word of truth" (2 Tim. 2:15), or they are comparing scripture to scripture. They don't recognize that they are seeing it incorrectly.

There is a teaching that says when we get saved or ask for forgiveness of sins, past, present, and future sins are automatically under the blood and forgiven. Have you ever heard that? The premise is that because Jesus died in the past for all sin in the future (and we are in the future) and (here is where the circular reasoning comes in) He automatically forgives all our sin—past, present, and future. Why would you have to ask in the first place if He has already forgiven it? The reasoning is not correct. There is no scripture that says past, present, and future sins are automatically under the blood when we ask for forgiveness and get saved. This is just not scriptural. We know John said in 1 John speaking to believers that if you confess your sin, He is faithful and just to forgive you.

I John 1:9

9 If we confess our sins, he is faithful and just to forgive us our sins, and to cleanse us from all unrighteousness.

Is there any of you who have never sinned since you have been saved? If past, present, and future sins are already under the blood, why would we have to confess them and get them forgiven and cleansed? It is already forgiven. The teaching develops into all kinds of concepts that are just not scriptural. You just go around in circles with the preconceived idea. Some have come up with the idea that you don't have to repent after you are saved because you are already cleansed. Then you end up getting further and further into false teaching, such as the idea that since Jesus died for everyone, then everyone is saved. No, that just is not true. Jesus' salvation is a gift we have to receive. The other one I have heard is that since we are cleansed from *all* unrighteousness that it, too, means past, present, and future sins. I have heard it said specifically "all" means past, present, and future. Where do those who say this get it? "All" doesn't mean past, present, and future. Say you are working on a bachelor's degree in college and you have two semesters to go, and you have a 4.0 average. At this point, you say, "I have all A's". Does that mean when you finish getting your degree two semesters later that you automatically have all A's? No. You could get a B or a C in those last semesters and lose your all A's. Another example is if you say, "My house is all clean. All the clothes are washed, all the dusting and vacuuming is done, and everything is straightened up." Does that mean a month from now it is still clean if you haven't touched the house? No, of course not. I reiterate, you will not find any scriptures that say that past, present, and future sins are under the blood. In 2 Peter 1:9, it states you are purged from your old sins. Romans 3:25 uses the phrase, "Sins that are *past.*"

This example of a false teaching demonstrates how a preconceived idea will create circular reasoning. You will look at a scripture, and you are blinded from the truth because you are accepting the preconceived idea. It is hard to see past that. It is also hard for anyone to show you past that. When you read a scripture, you will say, "This can't mean what it says because it doesn't fit the doctrine. Now that is all right, if the doctrine is correct. It may be that the wording of the scripture seems strange or your understanding is incorrect. You will tell yourself, "I must not understand what is being said." False doctrine is often based on scripture, and many would lay aside the false doctrine, if they knew it was incorrect. However, there are those who will insist on holding on to a teaching because it is a church doctrine or because the false doctrine sounds better or fits into their lifestyle in spite of what the scripture actually is saying. Jesus said:

Matthew 15:6 b

6   Thus have ye made the commandment of God
    of none effect by your tradition.

I have heard people say about some of Jesus' teachings that He didn't mean what He said. Jesus said if someone asks to borrow from you to lend and not expect it back (Luke 6:34). Some may say that Jesus couldn't mean that. Someone could step on us and take advantage. Yet He did mean what He said. If we obey it, then Jesus can take care of us and bless us if someone takes advantage. Someone once said, "If Jesus didn't mean what He said, I wish He had said what He meant because I believe what He said." There are times though, when we do need to seek for further understanding. He also said if we don't *hate* father and mother, we can't be His disciple (Luke 14:26). Matthew 10: 37 states it a different way. It says we are not to love father and mother *more* than Jesus. We come to understand that we are to put Jesus first above even our father and mother, yet we are still to honor them. So, the hate in Luke 24:16 means to love less.

One way you can recognize if a preconceived idea is based on false doctrine is when every scripture concerning it has to be changed in some way or explained to fit the doctrine. There has to be something wrong with the doctrine.

I was meditating one time on the fact that there are so many ministers used of God who see the rapture differently. I thought, *God, you had to have known that there would be confusion.* I realized that of course, He does know, so there must be a reason. Many times in scripture concerning end-times, we are told not to be deceived. Couldn't He have made it plainer? It doesn't seem that anyone has it altogether. All the puzzle pieces don't seem to fit.

Then I thought that first of all, if God had made it clearer, that with the Spirit of God in us, we could figure out the day and the hour. He does not want that; at least not yet. Then, too, Satan could use the information for his advantage, or people would be trying to hasten things or slow them down. We do not need to be concerned that no one knows.

The reason I was impressed to write this book is because it could soon be coming time for God to start putting it all together for us, and we need to be ready not only for the rapture but to receive revelation. This is why I cannot emphasize enough that we need to be ready: to watch, pray and not be so insistent we understand it all.

CHAPTER 2

The Rapture Defined

SCRIPTURES TELLING US WHAT OCCURS DURING THE RAPTURE

I Thessalonians 4: 13 – 18

13 But I would not have you to be ignorant, brethren, concerning them which are asleep, that ye sorrow not, even as others which have no hope.

14 For if we believe that Jesus died and rose again, even so them also which sleep in Jesus will God bring with him.

15 For this we say unto you by the word of the Lord, that we which are alive and remain unto the coming of the Lord shall not prevent them which are asleep.

16 For the Lord himself shall descend from heaven with a shout, with the voice of the archangel, and with the trump of God: and the dead in Christ shall rise first:

17 Then we which are alive and remain shall be caught up together with them in the clouds, to meet the Lord in the air: and so shall we ever be with the Lord.

18 Wherefore comfort one another with these words.

Verse 13. Paul speaks of them who are asleep. This refers to those in Christ (those that are saved) who have died.

Verses 14 – 15. Those who have died in the Lord and gone on to be with Jesus, He will bring back with Him at His coming. James 2:26 says that the body is dead without the spirit. It would take a long discussion to go through the references that show us that we are spirit, soul and body. We are spirit, we posses a soul which is our mind, will and emotions, and we live in a body. The body is our earth-suit. As a space-suit allows astronauts to walk around in space, this body, allows us to walk around on the earth. When we die, our spirit with the soul, leaves the body. The spirit of those who have died in the Lord (born-again believers) are with Jesus in heaven and when Jesus returns, He will bring those spirits with Him. There will be believers who are still alive and still here on the earth when Jesus returns.

Verses 16 – 17. At the coming of the Lord, the Lord shall descend, and there will be a trumpet sound. The dead in Christ shall rise first (their bodies will rise), and those born-again believers who are alive and remain shall be caught up together in the clouds to meet Jesus at His coming. We shall ever be with the Lord.

Resurrection of the Dead in Christ that Occurs at Christ's Coming.

I Corinthians 15: 20 – 23, 23, 50 – 53

20 But now is Christ risen from the dead, and become the firstfruits of them that slept.

22 For as in Adam all die, even so in Christ shall all be made alive

23 But every man in his own order: Christ the firstfruits; afterward they that are Christ's at his coming.

50 Now this I say, brethren, that flesh and blood cannot inherit the Kingdom of God; neither doth corruption inherit incorruption.

51 Behold, I shew you a mystery; We shall not all sleep, but we shall all be changed,

ked, and, behold, a door was
en: and the first voice which I
were of a trumpet talking with
, Come up hither, and I will shew
ich must be hereafter.

tely I was in the spirit: and,
one was set in heaven, and one
one.

g. Verse 2 says that John was in the spirit. In
elation, he says he was in the spirit on the
Jesus, and that is where the revelation begins.
hat he is in the spirit. Did he get a resurrected
ut on incorruption? No. Eventually, he comes
rites what he saw and heard. He doesn't get
question to ask, "Is there a coming of Christ?"
ure, there had to be a coming, and there isn't
ilar to when Paul was caught up into the third
realm where God dwells). He came back to
t the rapture.

pture, then to take that to its logical conclusion,
o one will be able to know what will come after
e rapture occurs because John is told that after
be shown what will happen afterwards. This is
re is.

ht by some, that the word, "church," is not
ook of Revelation after this verse, so the church
ptured and are in heaven for the rest of the book
specific word is not mentioned, but believers in
ned throughout the rest of Revelation. The word,
oned in the second and third chapter of Revelation
discussing seven specific churches in Asia. There
these two chapters for the specific word, "church"
word, "church," is also not mentioned in any
the rapture, but that does not mean believers do

---

52 In a moment, in the twinkling of an eye, at the
last trump: For the trumpet shall sound, and
the dead shall be raised incorruptible, and we
shall be changed.

53 For this corruptible must put on incorruption,
and this mortal must put on immortality.

Versus 20 – 23. The resurrection of the dead in Christ occurs *at His coming.* In verse 23, we see Christ the firstfruits. Afterward, they that are Christ's at His coming.

Some have said there are many resurrections before Christ's coming, but that is not what this scripture says. This says that Christ was the firstfruits, the first to be resurrected. Those who are asleep in Christ will be resurrected at His coming, not before. (Now the next scriptures explain that this is referring to the resurrection in which we put on an incorruptible, immortal body.) You may have heard of people in this life that were dead and came back to life, but they are not in their resurrected (immortal) body, and they will die again unless alive at the time of the rapture.

Verses 50 – 52. We shall be changed, in the twinkling of an eye. This means quickly, before you can blink. Someone has said faster than a thought. I have said faster than a nano-second, at the last trump. The last trump is significant. In the Book of Revelation, there is reference to many trumpets that sound. Being last means that nothing comes after.

Verse 53. Incorruption means a body that will not decay, and immortality means eternal. I will refer to this as a resurrected body. Some have called it a glorified body. The gospels speak of Jesus being "glorified" when He raises from the dead and ascends to heaven. It is a body that will never die. We can only imagine how wonderful this body will be. We will probably look as though we are in our twenties, and be perfect, never to get sick or wrinkled. If we were crippled or deformed in any way in this life, it will not be the case in our resurrected bodies.

WHAT OCCURS AT THE TIME OF THE RAPTURE?
(Now we can see specifically what happens at the rapture.)

- ✤ A coming of the Lord
- ✤ Trumpet sound, particularly the last trump
- ✤ Resurrection of the dead in Christ
- ✤ Gathering together of the dead in Christ rising with those who are alive and remain to meet Christ in the air at Christ's coming. All are instantly changed in a twinkling of the eye from corruption to incorruption, mortality to immortality. (Resurrected body)

I say *a* coming of the Lord because we will learn (and you may know this already) that *the* coming of the Lord is at the end of the Tribulation period when Jesus comes to the earth, and ends the battle of Armageddon. This battle will be discussed later. Born-again believers, the dead in Christ, whom Jesus has brought with Him (It will be explained later that when a person dies, his spirit leaves his body, and the born-again believer goes to heaven as a spirit to be with Christ,) and those in Christ who are alive on the earth have risen into the air to meet Him, will go with Him to that battle. He ends the battle and sets up His millennial (thousand year) reign. If the rapture is pre-trib, then there has to be *a* coming of the Lord in the air to take the church back to heaven until the Tribulation period is over. If I say *the* coming, I am referring to the coming of the Lord to the earth at the battle of Armageddon at the end of the Tribulation period. This coming is referred to as the Second Coming. All who believe in the Second Coming acknowledge that Jesus ends the battle of Armageddon at this coming, ending the Tribulation period and beginning His millennial reign. It is only the pre-trib doctrine that sets up a need for Christ to have another coming just in the air before His Second Coming.

When a pre-trib believer is reading a scripture that addresses the events of the rapture at the coming of the Lord, such as the first one in this chapter: I Thessalonians 4:13 – 18, the pre-trib belief requires the explanation that the coming referred to in that scripture cannot be Jesus' Second Coming, but a different coming. This is because if

52 In a moment, in the twinkling of an eye, at the
last trump: For the trumpet shall sound, and
the dead shall be raised incorruptible, and we
shall be changed.

53 For this corruptible must put on incorruption,
and this mortal must put on immortality.

Versus 20 – 23. The resurrection of the dead in Christ occurs *at His coming.* In verse 23, we see Christ the firstfruits. Afterward, they that are Christ's at His coming.

Some have said there are many resurrections before Christ's coming, but that is not what this scripture says. This says that Christ was the firstfruits, the first to be resurrected. Those who are asleep in Christ will be resurrected at His coming, not before. (Now the next scriptures explain that this is referring to the resurrection in which we put on an incorruptible, immortal body.) You may have heard of people in this life that were dead and came back to life, but they are not in their resurrected (immortal) body, and they will die again unless alive at the time of the rapture.

Verses 50 – 52. We shall be changed, in the twinkling of an eye. This means quickly, before you can blink. Someone has said faster than a thought. I have said faster than a nano-second, at the last trump. The last trump is significant. In the Book of Revelation, there is reference to many trumpets that sound. Being last means that nothing comes after.

Verse 53. Incorruption means a body that will not decay, and immortality means eternal. I will refer to this as a resurrected body. Some have called it a glorified body. The gospels speak of Jesus being "glorified" when He raises from the dead and ascends to heaven. It is a body that will never die. We can only imagine how wonderful this body will be. We will probably look as though we are in our twenties, and be perfect, never to get sick or wrinkled. If we were crippled or deformed in any way in this life, it will not be the case in our resurrected bodies.

WHAT OCCURS AT THE TIME OF THE RAPTURE?
(Now we can see specifically what happens at the rapture.)

✦ A coming of the Lord
✦ Trumpet sound, particularly the last trump
✦ Resurrection of the dead in Christ
✦ Gathering together of the dead in Christ rising with those who are alive and remain to meet Christ in the air at Christ's coming. All are instantly changed in a twinkling of the eye from corruption to incorruption, mortality to immortality. (Resurrected body)

I say *a* coming of the Lord because we will learn (and you may know this already) that *the* coming of the Lord is at the end of the Tribulation period when Jesus comes to the earth, and ends the battle of Armageddon. This battle will be discussed later. Born-again believers, the dead in Christ, whom Jesus has brought with Him (It will be explained later that when a person dies, his spirit leaves his body, and the born-again believer goes to heaven as a spirit to be with Christ,) and those in Christ who are alive on the earth have risen into the air to meet Him, will go with Him to that battle. He ends the battle and sets up His millennial (thousand year) reign. If the rapture is pre-trib, then there has to be *a* coming of the Lord in the air to take the church back to heaven until the Tribulation period is over. If I say *the* coming, I am referring to the coming of the Lord to the earth at the battle of Armageddon at the end of the Tribulation period. This coming is referred to as the Second Coming. All who believe in the Second Coming acknowledge that Jesus ends the battle of Armageddon at this coming, ending the Tribulation period and beginning His millennial reign. It is only the pre-trib doctrine that sets up a need for Christ to have another coming just in the air before His Second Coming.

When a pre-trib believer is reading a scripture that addresses the events of the rapture at the coming of the Lord, such as the first one in this chapter: I Thessalonians 4:13 – 18, the pre-trib belief requires the explanation that the coming referred to in that scripture cannot be Jesus' Second Coming, but a different coming. This is because if it is referring to Jesus' actual Second Coming, it would mean the rapture would have to be occurring post-trib, since that is when Jesus' Second coming actually occurs. Hence, since the particular scripture is referring to the rapture at His coming, and the pre-trib rapture belief is that the rapture occurs before the tribulation, not after the tribulation at Jesus' Second Coming, the scripture has to be referring to another coming of Jesus. Do you detect a circular reasoning?

There is a trumpet sound, and we know, according to 1 Corinthians 15, it is referred to as the last trump. There is a resurrection of the dead in Christ, and the living who are in Christ are caught up together with the dead in Christ, and we are all changed to a resurrected body.

The word *rapture* is not in the KJV and other translations. It is from a word in the Latin Vulgate (an old manuscript). As long as we understand the event that is being called the rapture, it doesn't matter. The event will be rapturous. This event has also been called a "catching away" a reference to 1 Thessalonians 4 being "caught up together." I like to use the phrase "gathering together" because we will see this terminology in many scriptures as in 2 Thessalonians, in the gospels and in the book of Revelation.

Any time when one is referring to a scripture and says, "We (speaking of born-again Christians) aren't here for this scripture because the rapture has already taken place," or a particular scripture is referring to the rapture, then we must ask, "Have the criteria for a rapture taken place?" Has Christ come? Has the resurrection of the dead in Christ occurred? Are born-again believers in their resurrected bodies?

It seems that as I have listened to teachings, many try to find the rapture in countless places. It seems they want so much to find where the rapture is that they will make up places. For example, in Rev. 4 John is told, "Come up hither." Many have said that this is where the rapture occurs because the rest of Revelation is referring to the Tribulation period. It is said that this is a type of rapture. But read what it says:

Revelation 4: 1-2

1   After this I looked, and, behold, a door was opened in heaven: and the first voice which I heard was as it were of a trumpet talking with me; which said, *Come up hither, and I will shew thee things which must be hereafter.*

2   And immediately I was in the spirit: and, behold, a throne was set in heaven, and one sat on the throne.

This is John speaking. Verse 2 says that John was in the spirit. In the first chapter of Revelation, he says he was in the spirit on the Lord's Day, and he sees Jesus, and that is where the revelation begins. Here, too, he is saying that he is in the spirit. Did he get a resurrected body? Did corruption put on incorruption? No. Eventually, he comes back to himself and writes what he saw and heard. He doesn't get resurrected. The other question to ask, "Is there a coming of Christ?" No. If there was a rapture, there had to be a coming, and there isn't that either. This is similar to when Paul was caught up into the third heaven (the spiritual realm where God dwells). He came back to himself, and it wasn't the rapture.

If it is a type of rapture, then to take that to its logical conclusion, it would mean that no one will be able to know what will come after the rapture until the rapture occurs because John is told that after he goes up, he will be shown what will happen afterwards. This is not where the rapture is.

It is also taught by some, that the word, "church," is not mentioned in the book of Revelation after this verse, so the church must have been raptured and are in heaven for the rest of the book of Revelation. The specific word is not mentioned, but believers in Christ are mentioned throughout the rest of Revelation. The word, "church," is mentioned in the second and third chapter of Revelation because Jesus is discussing seven specific churches in Asia. There is no need, after these two chapters for the specific word, "church" to be used. The word, "church," is also not mentioned in any scripture about the rapture, but that does not mean believers do